WAS IST LERNEN AN STATIONEN?

Beim Lernen an Stationen handelt es sich um eine Form selbstständigen Arbeitens, bei der
- ☐ unterschiedliche Lernvoraussetzungen,
- ☐ unterschiedliche Zugänge und Betrachtungsweisen,
- ☐ unterschiedliches Lern- und Arbeitstempo
- ☐ und häufig fächerübergreifendes Arbeiten

berücksichtigt werden.

Grundidee

Den Schülerinnen und Schülern werden Arbeitsstationen zur individuellen Bearbeitung angeboten, an welchen sie selbstständig, in beliebiger Abfolge und meist auch in frei gewählter Sozialform entsprechend ihren Möglichkeiten und Fähigkeiten arbeiten. Damit soll ihnen optimales Lernen und Üben ermöglicht werden.

Herkunft und Entwicklung

Die Idee des Lernens an Stationen, auch Lernzirkel genannt, kommt ursprünglich aus dem Sportbereich. Das „circuit training", von Morgan und Adamson 1952 in England entwickelt, stellt den Sportlern unterschiedliche Übungsstationen zur Verfügung, die sie der Reihe nach oder in freier Auswahl durchlaufen.
Eine Übertragung dieser Lernform auf Unterrichtsinhalte in verschiedenen Fächern wurde zunächst an der Schallenbergschule in Aidlingen/Baden-Württemberg, später am Seminar für schulpraktische Ausbildung in Sindelfingen und an vielen Schulen seit etwa 1980 aufgegriffen und stetig weiterentwickelt.
Der Herausgeber und die Autoren stellen die Ergebnisse ihrer eigenen praktischen Arbeit und Erfahrung in dieser Reihe vor und bieten ihre Materialien als Grundlage für den direkten Einsatz oder als Grundlage für eine Anpassung an eigene Bedürfnisse an.

Zielrichtungen

Das Lernen an Stationen kann unterschiedliche Ziele verfolgen:
- ☐ Optimales Üben ermöglichen durch ein breites Angebot, das die verschiedenen Lerneingangskanäle, allgemeine Übungsgesetze, unterschiedliche Aufgabenarten, Schwierigkeiten und Hilfestellungen berücksichtigt.
- ☐ Vertiefendes Bearbeiten eines Inhalts beziehungsweise eines Themengebietes, indem Schülerinnen und Schüler nach zuvor gestalteter Übersicht oder Einführung die Inhalte auf ihre Art, mit ihren Möglichkeiten und in ihrem individuellen Tempo auf unterschiedlichen Ebenen selbstständig bearbeiten.
- ☐ Selbstständiges Erarbeiten von Themengebieten, indem die Schülerinnen und Schüler durch angemessene Arbeitsangebote Sachverhalte hinterfragen, erforschen, erfahren, gestalten usw.
- ☐ Angebote aus Schulbüchern oder Medien unter ganzheitlicher Betrachtungsweise aufarbeiten, indem die Schülerinnen und Schüler Aufgabenstellungen zu Teilgebieten mit unterschiedlicher Betrachtungsweise und auf unterschiedlichen Ebenen fächerübergreifend bearbeiten.

Organisation

Die einzelnen Arbeitsaufträge geben den Schülerinnen und Schülern klare oder offene Aufgabenstellungen mit eindeutigen Anweisungen. Die Angebote werden im Klassenzimmer zur Verfügung gestellt, indem der Arbeitsauftrag durch Aushängen oder Auslegen bereitgestellt wird. Dazu bietet sich zum Schutz das Verpacken in Prospekthüllen an.
Als Ort zum Aushängen eignen sich alle Wand- und zum Teil auch die Fensterflächen. Pinn-Nadeln oder Nägel (Nagelleisten) erleichtern das Aufhängen und Abnehmen. Beim Auslegen der Arbeitsangebote bzw. -aufträge helfen Ablagekörbe, Ordnung zu halten.
Das Bereitstellen außerhalb der Schülerarbeitstische (also auf Fensterbänken, Nebentischen oder durch Aufhängen) erübrigt das tägliche Aufbauen und Wiederabräumen, stellt also eine große zeitliche und organisatorische Erleichterung dar. Falls im „Fachlehrerbetrieb" der ständige Abbau nötig ist, sind ineinander stapelbare Ablagekörbe, in welchen die Aufträge verbleiben, sehr hilfreich.
Die Kennzeichnung der einzelnen Stationen durch Ziffern, Buchstaben oder Symbole hilft den Schülerinnen und Schülern bei der Orientierung. Durch bewusste Verwendung dieser Ordnungsangebote kann die Struktur des Themengebietes oder eine andere Struktur (z. B. Arbeitsform o. Ä.) gleichzeitig verdeutlicht werden.

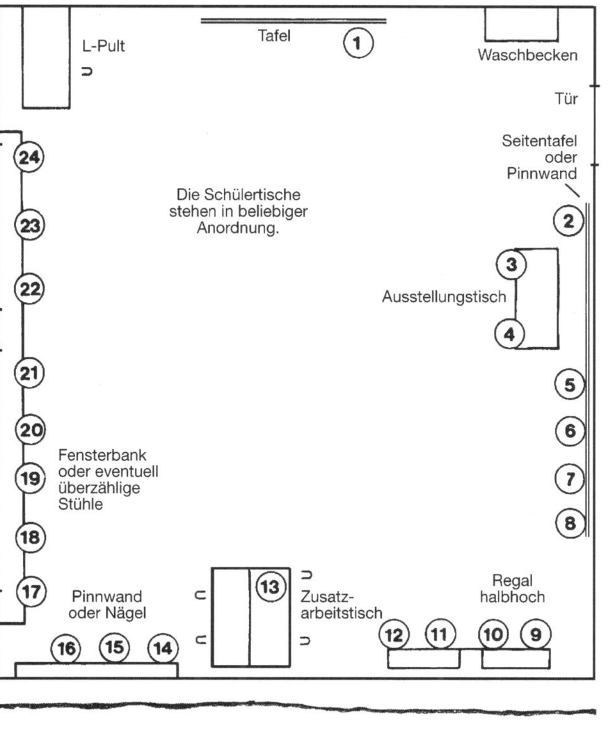

Eine Fortschrittsliste bzw. ein Laufzettel gibt Schülerinnen und Schülern wie den Lehrkräften jederzeit eine Rückmeldung über den derzeitigen Bearbeitungsstand und dient der Übersicht.

Auswahlangebote

Den Schülerinnen und Schülern ist sinnvollerweise ein Auswahlangebot zu ermöglichen; Minimalanforderungen können von der Lehrerin oder dem Lehrer definiert werden. Als Orientierungshilfe finden Sie dazu in den Hinweisen zu diesem Themenheft weitere Angaben.

Sonstige Tipps

Organisatorische Bedingungen und Festlegungen sind möglichst an der konkreten Situation und erst beim tatsächlichen Bedarf zu klären und zu regeln. Ist die Klassenstärke größer als die Anzahl der zur Verfügung stehenden Arbeitsstationen, können Sie die einzelnen Arbeitsaufträge mehrfach anfertigen. Weitere Hinweise zur Organisation, zu den Inhalten und zum Lernen an Stationen allgemein finden Sie im Einführungsband zu dieser Reihe, der unter dem Titel *Schülergerechtes Arbeiten in der Sekundarstufe I: Lernen an Stationen* im selben Verlag erschienen ist.

Roland Bauer
(Herausgeber)

ALLGEMEINE HINWEISE ZU DIESEM THEMENHEFT

Die vorliegenden Stationen sind zum einen in die inhaltlichen Bereiche *Buildings and Sights*, *Places*, *Shopping* und *Transport* unterteilt, zum anderen aber auch in die Lernbereiche Vokabeln, Landeskunde, Textarbeit, *Conversation* und Spiele untergliedert.
Daraus ergibt sich folgende Matrix:

	A **Sights and buildings**	**B** **Places**	**C** **Shopping**	**D** **Transport**
1. Vokabeln	Sights and buildings	Where can a place be?	Shops in the city	The vehicle puzzle
2. Landeskunde	What to see in London	A map of London	Street markets	Going by Underground
3. Textarbeit	London – where the tourists go	Streets of London	Harrods	In the Underground
4. Conversation	Buying an entrance ticket	Telling the way	Let's go shopping	Asking for information and buying a ticket
5. Spiele	The London Sights Quiz	Getting around	A shopping game	A tour through London

Diese Matrix erlaubt es, auch nur einen Lernbereich, wie z.B. Vokabeln herauszugreifen, der dann nach und nach durch alle vier inhaltlichen Bereiche hindurch geführt werden kann (*Sights and buildings*, *Places*, *Shopping* und *Transport*).
Bei der Erstellung dieser Stationen wurden die verschiedenen Lerntypen ebenso berücksichtigt wie unterschiedliche Methoden und Lerntechniken. Die Stationen lassen die unterschiedlichsten Sozialformen zu, von Einzel-, über Partner- bis zu Gruppenarbeit.
Zur besseren Orientierung empfiehlt es sich, alle Stationen eines inhaltlichen Bereichs (*Sights and buildings*, *Places*, *Shopping* und *Transport*) jeweils auf gleichfarbiges Papier zu kopieren. Selbstverständlich kann mit den Arbeitsblättern und selbst erstellten Materialien auch ein London-Buch zusammengestellt werden.
Die Lösungsblätter sollten auf jeden Fall getrennt von den Stationen aufbewahrt werden, z.B. an der Tafel oder einer Pinnwand.

MATERIALLISTE UND ANMERKUNGEN

LAUFZETTEL VON: ....

Die folgenden Stationen habe ich schon geschafft:

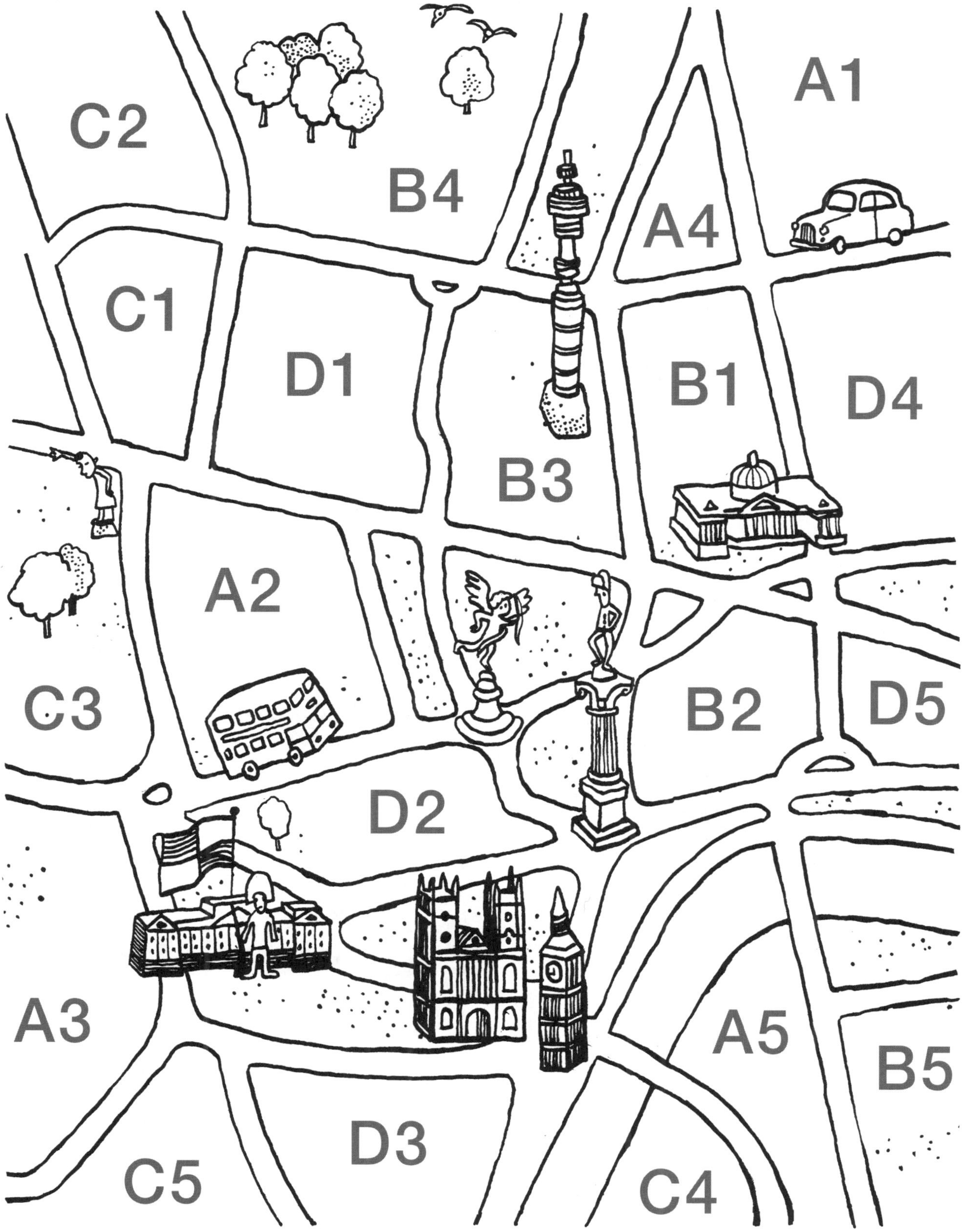

A MAP OF LONDON • A MAP OF LONDON

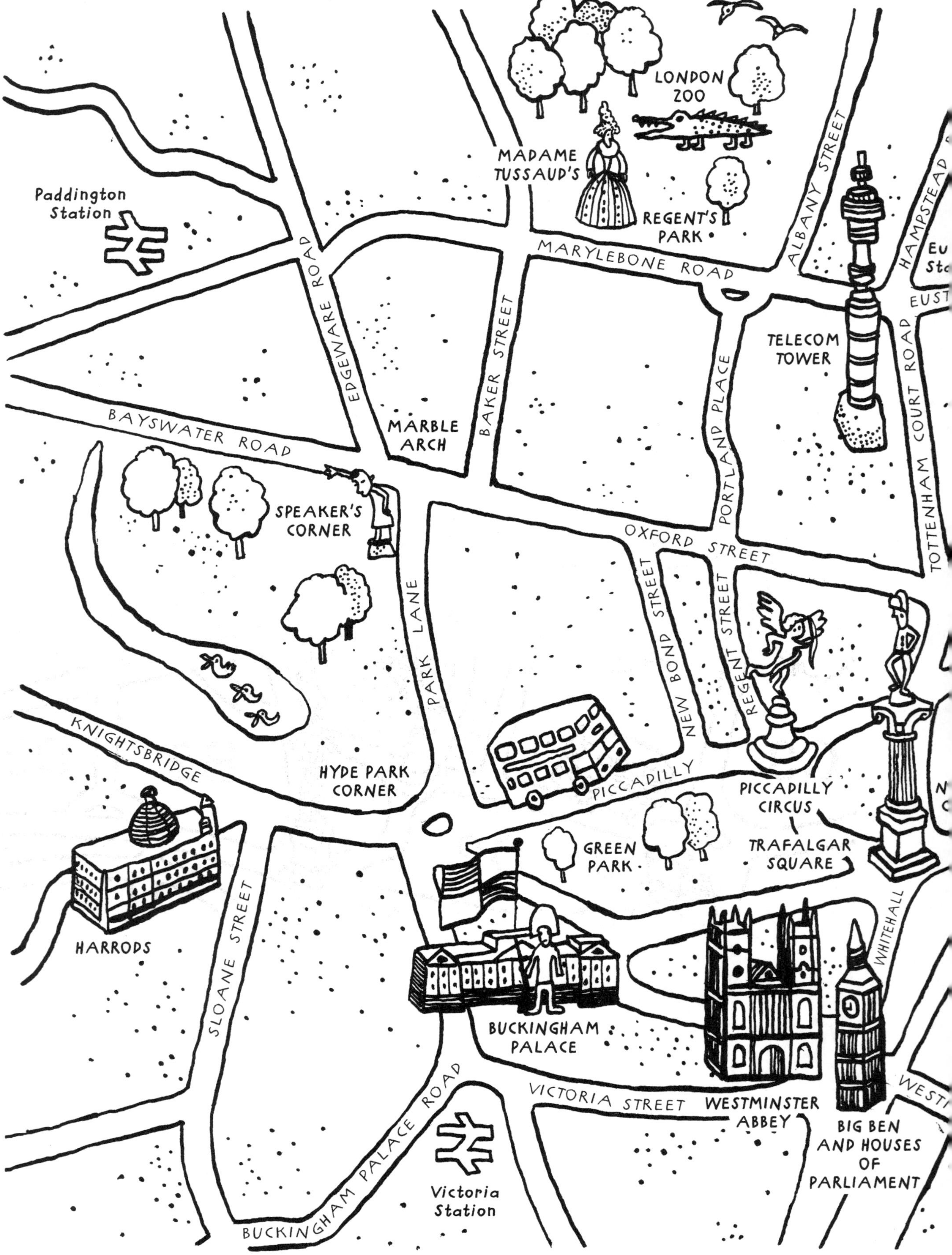

A MAP OF LONDON • A MAP OF LONDON

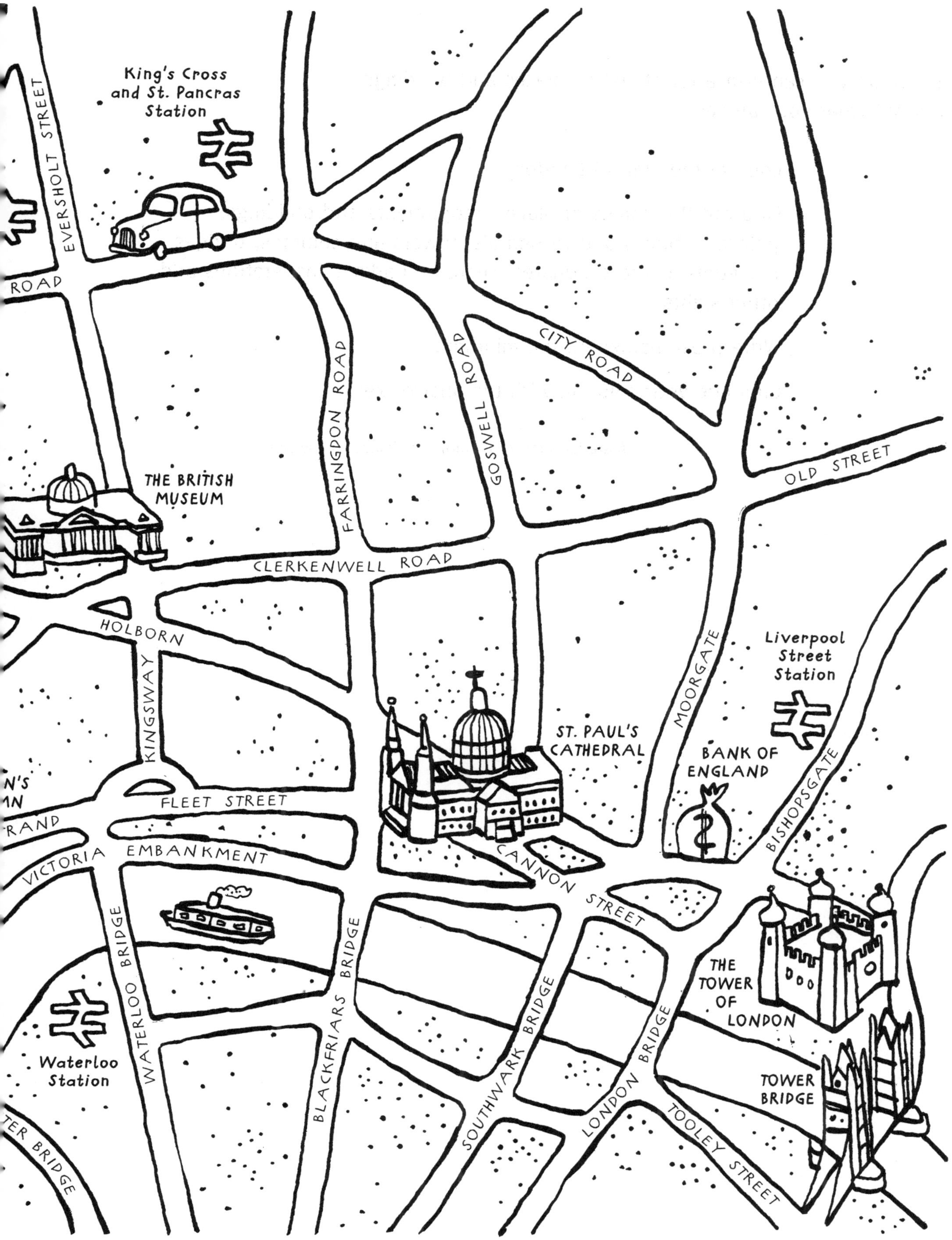

SIGHTS AND BUILDINGS

In London you can visit a lot of sights, places and buildings.
Find out what you can see.

- Look at the map of London.
- Find out the names of places, monuments and buildings, palaces, abbeys and cathedrals, towers and columns, bridges, museums, corners, squares, circuses, parks, zoos, stations and other sights
- Write those names on the mindmap.
- Compare your solution with the answer key.

Material: map of London, worksheet, answer key

MINDMAP WORKSHEET

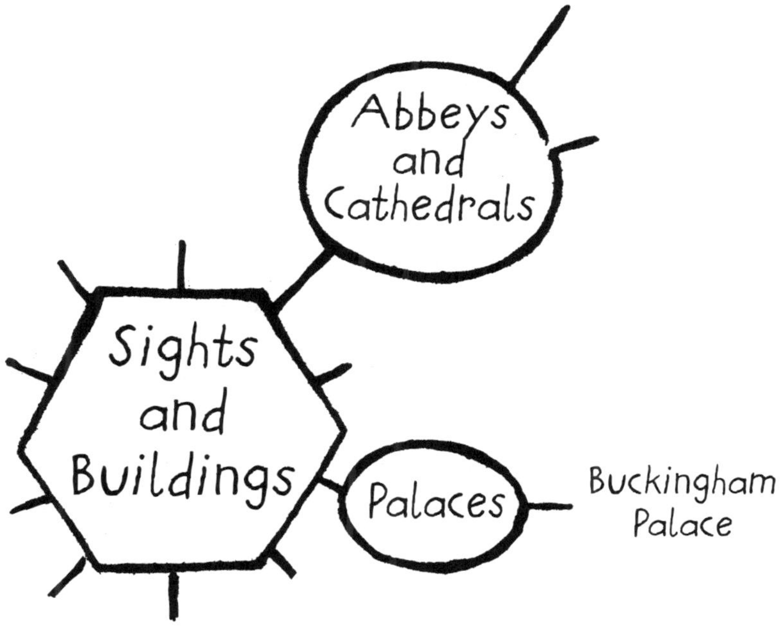

MINDMAP ANSWER KEY

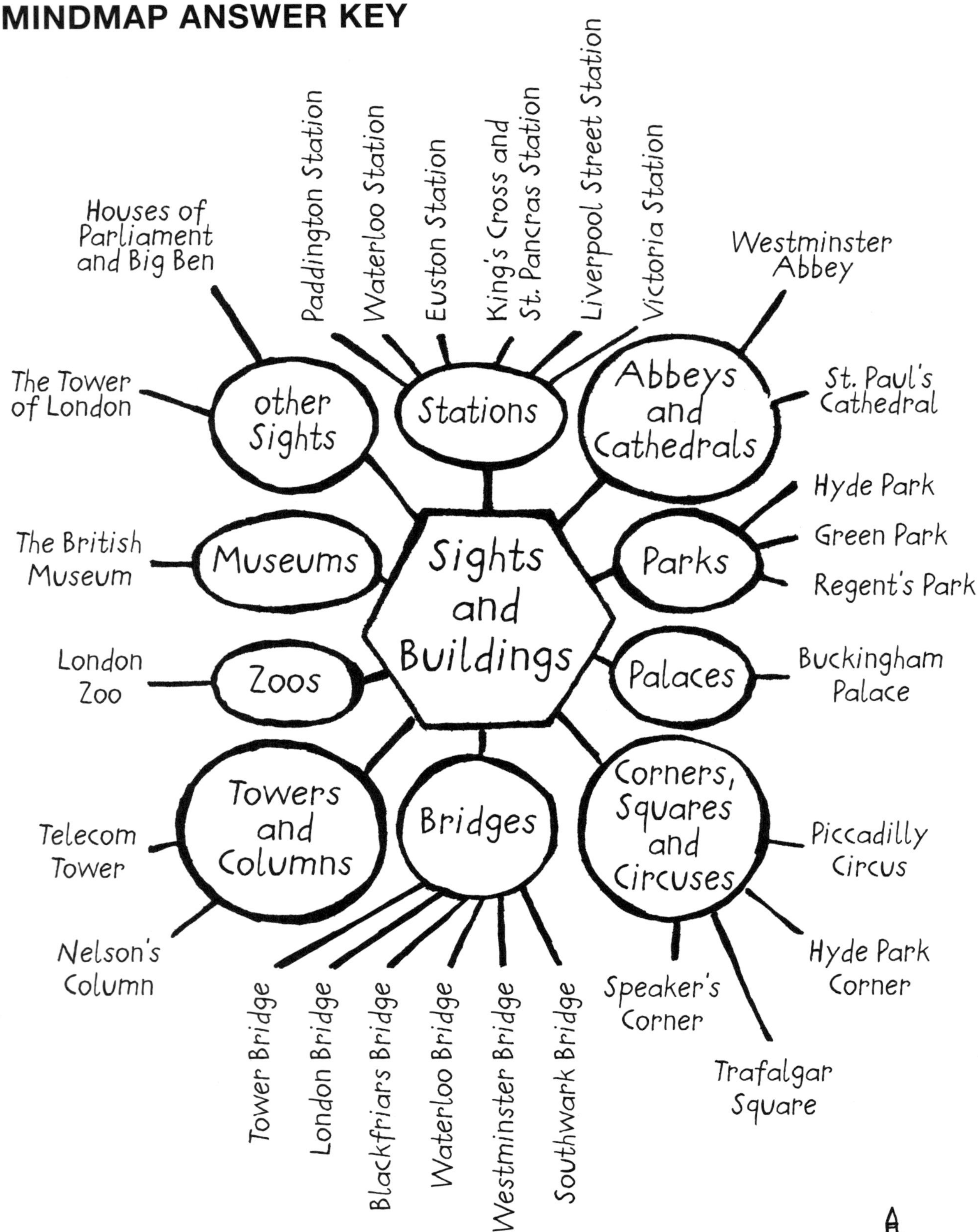

WHAT I WOULD LIKE TO SEE IN LONDON

You are going to visit London! What sights would you like to see?
Plan your own sightseeing tour.

- Look at the map of London.
- You can prepare your own worksheet to plan your sightseeing tour:
  - Write down the sights you would like to see on your sheet of paper.
  - Try to find pictures of the sights you have chosen. Cut out the pictures and glue them onto the worksheet.
  - Look for further information about your chosen sights in travel brochures, travel guide books, your schoolbooks ...
  - Write down the information on your worksheet.
- Present your own sightseeing tour to your class.

Material: map of London (s. pages 6/7), blank sheets of paper, scissors, glue, pictures (photocopies) from London-travel-guide-books and travel brochures for London etc.

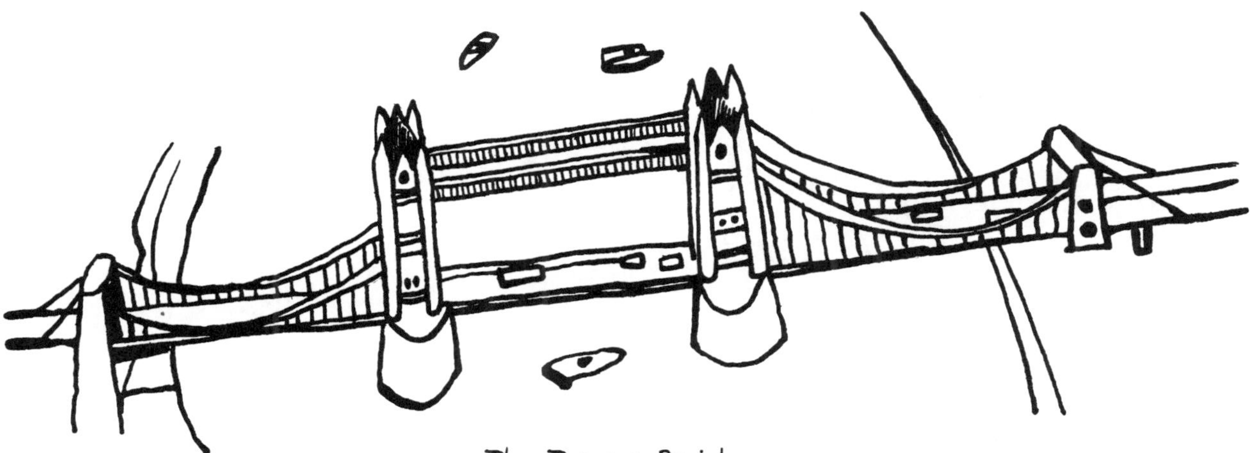

The Tower Bridge

WHERE THE TOURISTS GO

In London there are very famous places where you can find a lot of tourists.

- Read the text "London: Where the tourists go".
- Look up the unknown words in your dictionary.
  Write these words in alphabetical order in your exercise book.
- On your worksheet there are true and false statements.
  Mark the true statements.
- Try to find these sights on your map.
- Compare your solutions with the answer key.

Material: text "London: Where the tourists go", dictionary, worksheet, answer key

WHERE THE TOURISTS GO – TEXT

London: Where the tourists go

We can start in Westminster, at the Houses of Parliament. Do you know what Big Ben is? Is it the name of the tower, the clock on the tower, or the big bell inside the clock tower? Well, people sometimes call the clock and even the tower Big Ben, but it is really the name of the huge bell. (It weighs 13 1/2 tons.) You can hear Big Ben on the BBC World Service in almost every country in the world.

Now let's go along Whitehall to Trafalgar Square. Then we can walk along the Strand and Fleet Street to St. Paul's Cathedral, where Prince Charles and Princess Diana got married in 1981. St. Paul's is the second largest church in the world. Christopher Wren built it after the Great Fire of London in 1666. When you climb to the top of St. Paul's, you have got a wonderful view over London. From the top of St. Paul's to the ground it is 365 feet – one foot for every day of the year.

From St. Paul's it is not very far to the Tower of London. The Tower is over 900 years old and is one of the most famous castles in Britain. It was once a royal palace, the home of the kings and queens of England. Later it was a prison and a place for many executions. Some people say there are still ghosts in the Tower. Today it is a museum and over two million people visit it every year. They come to see the Crown Jewels and the Beefeaters.

Now let's go back to the West End and take the Underground to Baker Street. From there it is a one-minute walk to Madame Tussaud's with its wax figures of kings, queens, pop stars, politicians and – in the Chamber of Horrors – famous criminals. (Many years ago a criminal even sent his clothes to Madame Tussaud's on the day of his execution.) And when you see some of the big names from history, you will be surprised how small many of them really were!

Perhaps you'd like to go on a boat trip along the River Thames? From Westminster Pier, for example, you can travel down past the Tower and Greenwich to one of the most unusual tourist attractions in the world: the Thames Flood Barrier. In the past there have been several terrible floods in London. They can happen when the wind pushes the sea up the river towards London. There are walls along the river, but these are not high enough to protect the city. In 1928 fourteen people died when the water came over the walls in Westminster. A really bad flood might kill thousands of people and damage many of the historical buildings. Londoners now hope that the huge Thames Barrier will hold back the water so that this will never happen.

WHERE THE TOURISTS GO – WORKSHEET

1. Big Ben is ...
   A ☐ the tower of the Houses of Parliament.
   B ☐ the clock on the tower.
   C ☐ the big bell inside the clock tower.

2. St. Paul's Cathedral is ...
   A ☐ the church which was built for the wedding of Prince Charles in 1981.
   B ☐ the world's second largest church.
   C ☐ the church where Christopher Wren married.

3. The Tower of London was ...
   A ☐ a bridge.
   B ☐ a palace and a prison, but is a museum now.
   C ☐ the home of Queen Elizabeth I.

4. Madame Tussaud's is ...
   A ☐ a museum of wax figures.
   B ☐ a prison for famous criminals.
   C ☐ a historical place.

5. The Thames Flood Barrier is ...
   A ☐ a wall along the river.
   B ☐ a bad flood.
   C ☐ a barrier to hold back the water when the wind pushes it up the river towards London.

BUYING AN ENTRANCE TICKET

You are standing in front of the Tower of London and you want to buy an entrance ticket.

- Complete the following conversation with the cashier.
- The sentences given will help you.
- Compare your answers with the answer key.
- Learn the sentences and act out the scene with a partner

Good Morning! ______________________

______________________ "How old are you?"

______________________ "Are you a pupil?"

______________________ "Are you in a group?"

______________________ "Here is your ticket."

______________________ "It's £ 3.00."

Thank you. Good bye!

Material: answer key

Use these sentences: How much is it? / Here you are. / No, I'm alone. / Yes, I am. / I'd like a ticket for today / I'm 12/13/14 years old.

THE LONDON SIGHTS QUIZ

What do you know about the London sights?

- Put the triangles together.
- On one side of a triangle a sentence starts with the name of a sight. On a second triangle you have to find the correct second half of the sentence. Put the triangles together so that you can read the whole sentence.
- If you put all the triangles together correctly they will make up a bigger triangle again.
- Compare your solution with the answer key.

Material: Trimino, answer key

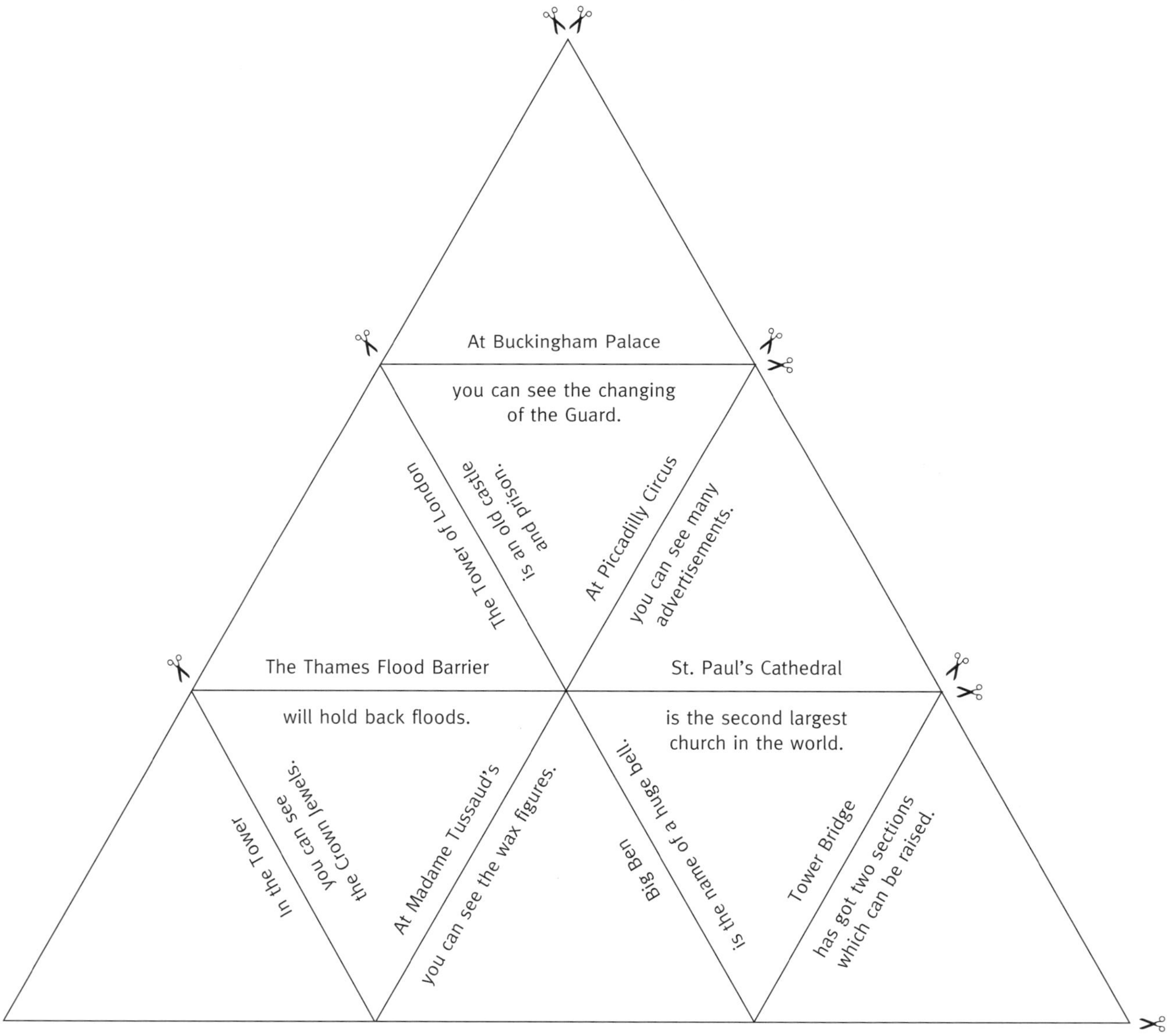

PLACES

STATION B1

WHERE CAN A PLACE BE?

Some sights, buildings and places in London are not far away from each other.

- Look at the worksheet. Describe the position of the buildings. Look up the words in your dictionary if you don't know them.
- Write the correct word under each picture.
- Compare your solution with the answer key.

Now have a look at the map of London again. There are a lot of sights in London. Can you say where they are?

Next to, opposite, behind, in front of, in the middle of ...

- Find yourself a partner. Take turns to ask a question (= taking a question-card) and answer the question.

Material: worksheet, question-cards, map of London (s. pages 6/7), answer key

WHERE CAN A PLACE BE? – WORKSHEET

1 neben

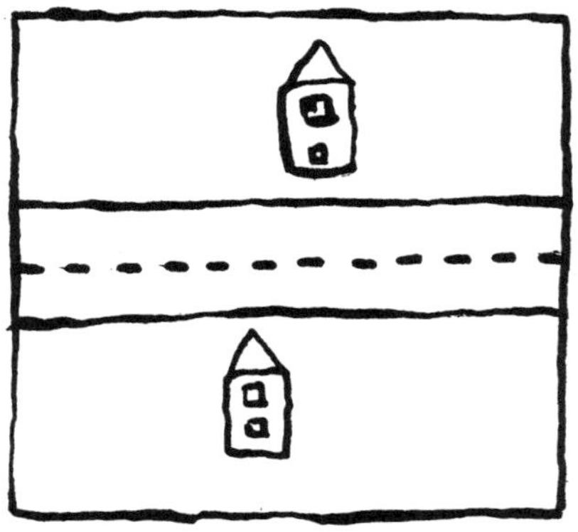

2 gegenüber

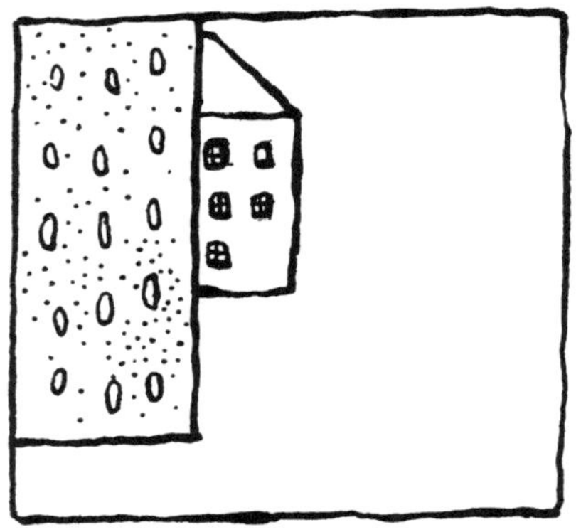

3 hinter

4 vor

5 in der Mitte von/inmitten

6 zwischen

7 an

8 nahe

9 links/rechts

PLACES

WHERE CAN A PLACE BE?
QUESTION- AND ANSWER-CARDS

Excuse me, where is Marble Arch?	Marble Arch is opposite Speaker's Corner (Hyde Park).
Excuse me, where is St. Paul's Cathedral?	St. Paul's Cathedral is near the Bank of England.
Excuse me, where is Big Ben?	Big Ben is next to the Houses of Parliament.
Excuse me, where is Westminster Abbey?	Westminster Abbey is between Buckingham Palace and Big Ben.
Excuse me, where is Tower Bridge?	Tower Bridge is near the Tower. Tower Bridge is near London Bridge.
Excuse me, where is the Tower?	The Tower is near Tower Bridge. The Tower is on the river Thames.

A MAP OF LONDON

Official town maps have got grid squares (= Planquadrate).
To find a sight or place ... you have to look for the letter and the number.
Try to read the town map.

- Work with a partner
- You can find the sights in several grid squares
- Tell your partner five sights (e.g. Westminster Abbey). He or she has to find the correct grid square. Change roles!
- Then do it the other way round: Tell your partner a grid square and then he has to name a sight in this square.

Material: map of London (s. pages 6/7) with grid squares

STREETS OF LONDON

"Streets of London" is a famous song by Ralph McTell. While walking through London he observes people.

- Listen to the song on the cassette/read the text.
- Did you understand the text?
- Put the text in the right order and read it.
- Draw, paint ... a picture illustrating the song.

Material: cassette, cassette-recorder, Puzzle with songtext, colour pencils, ..., paper

"STREETS OF LONDON" – LYRICS

The Streets of London

Have you seen the old man in the closed down market, kicking up the paper with his worn-out shoes?
In his eyes you see no pride, hands held loosely at his side, yesterday's paper telling yesterday's news.
So how can you tell me you're lonely, and say for you that the sun don't shine?
Let me take you by the hand and lead you through the Streets of London.
I'll show you something to make you change your mind.
Have you seen the old girl who walks the streets of London, dirt in her hair and her clothes in rags?
She's no time for talking she just keeps right on walking, carrying her home in two carrier bags.
So how can you tell me ...
In the all night café at a quarter past eleven, same old man sitting there on his own.
Looking at the world over the rim of his tea cup each tea lasts an hour and he wanders home alone.
So how can you tell me ...
Have you seen the old man outside the seamen's mission, memory fading with the medal ribbons that he wears?
And in our winter city the rain cries a little pity, for one more forgotten hero and a world that doesn't care.

TELLING THE WAY

- Work with a partner.
- First your partner takes the town map and you take one of the instruction-cards.
- Read the instructions on the card to your partner. Your partner has to follow your instructions. If he does so correctly he will end in front of the sight which is written on your card.
- Change roles now. You take the map, your partner takes another instruction-card and reads it to you.

Notice:

Go straight on	– gehe geradeaus
Turn right into	– biege rechts ein, in die ...
Turn left into	– biege links ein in die ...
Go along	– gehe ... entlang
Cross	– überquere

Material: map of London (s. pages 6/7), work sheet

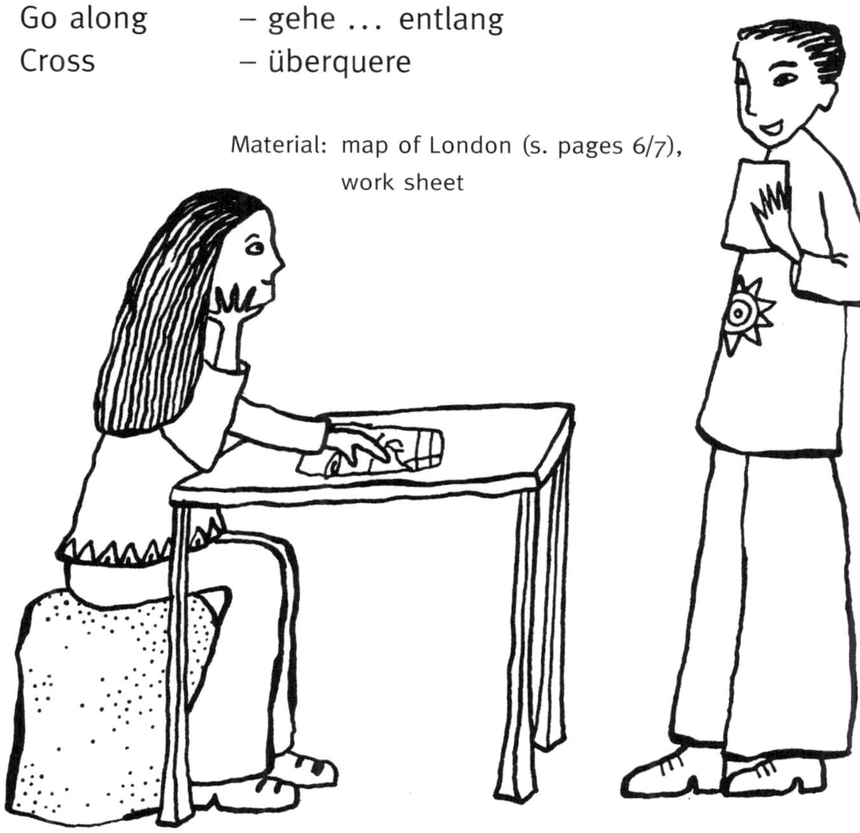

TELLING THE WAY – INSTRUCTION-CARDS

Imagine you are standing at Victoria Station.
Go along Buckingham Palace Road.
Turn right at Hyde Park Corner.
Go along Piccadilly.
At Piccadilly Circus you turn left into Regent Street.
Cross Oxford Street.
Go along Portland Place.
Turn left into Marylebone Road.
There is a museum on the right hand side. What is it called?

Madame Tussaud's

Imagine you are standing at Euston Station.
Go along Eversholt Street.
Cross Euston Road.
Continue going along Eversholt Street.
Turn left at Clerkenwell Road.
Turn right into Farringdon Road.
Go along Farringdon Road.
Cross Holborn Street.
Turn left into Cannon Street.
There is a huge church on the left hand side. What is it called?

St. Paul's Cathedral

GETTING AROUND

Send your partner on a sightseeing tour through London.

- Find yourself a partner. Both of you take a copy of a town map of London.
- Don't let your partner look at your map. Don't look at his/her map.
- Decide where you want to send your partner and from where you want to start. Mark both points on your map.
- Tell your partner step by step the way to the place or sight you have chosen for him/her.
- Has your partner found the place or sight? If so, change roles. It's his/her turn to send you to another place in London.

Material: two copies of the map (s. pages 6/7)

SHOPPING

STATION C1

SHOPS IN THE CITY

London is famous for shopping. Oxford Street for example is London's busiest shopping street.

- Write down all the kinds of shops you know.
  Tip: Look up the unknown words in your dictionary.
  Here are some things you would like to buy in London:
  Schuhe, Tee, Bücher, Pullover, Schokolade, Postkarten, Zeitschriften, CDs, Pommes Frites, Saft, Disketten, Poster, einen Stadtplan, Kekse ...
  But in what kind of shops would you buy these things?
- Write the name of the shops (e.g. bookshop) into the grid. Write down each letter of the words in squares. You can fill in the words horizontally, vertically or diagonally

											B			
B		B	O	O	K	S	H	O	P		O			
	O										O			
		O									K			
			K								S			
				S							H			

- After filling in all the words, let your teacher have a look at your worksheet. Note down your words at the bottom of the page. Then fill up the rest of the squares with other letters, so that your partner can't find your words all at once.
- Put the sheet into a clear plastic folder and ask your partner to find the words and mark them.
- After finding and marking all the words, clean the clear plastic folder, please!

Material: dictionary, worksheet, clear plastic folders, foil felt-tip-pens, cloth or sponge

SHOPPING

STATION C1

SHOPS IN THE CITY – WORKSHEET

									B					
									U					
									T					
									C					
									H					
									E					
									R					

Words to find: BUTCHER

STREET MARKETS

Beside the numerous shops there are street markets in London, too.

- Look at the information sheet about the street markets.
- What street market would you like to visit in London? What things can you buy in the various street markets?
  Tip: If you don't know the English word for something you would like to buy: Just look it up in the dictionary.
- Write an advertisement for (or create one with pictures of) your chosen street market.
  Tip: You can make a collage with pictures, photos ..., too.

Material: dictionary, paper, colour pencils, pictures, photos ...

London Street Markets – information sheet

Name/how to get there	**is open on**	**specialises in**
Portobello Market/ Tube: Notting Hill	Saturdays	antiques
Brixton Market/ British Rail: Brixton	Monday – Saturday	Caribbean-style fruit, vegetables
Leadenhall Market/ Tube: Bank	Monday – Friday	meat, poultry, vegetables
Petticoat Lane/ Tube: Aldgate	Sundays	clothes, knickknacks *(Krimskrams)*
Berwick Street Market/ Tube: Oxford Circus	Monday – Saturday	fruit, vegetables

SHOPPING

STATION C3

HARRODS

There is a very famous department store in London – HARRODS.

- Listen to the text.
- Listen to the text again: fill in the missing words into the gaps and answer the questions on the text.
- Compare your solution with the answer key.

Material: text, cassette, cassette recorder, worksheet (p.30), answer key

HARRODS – WORKSHEET

Harrods

Although there is a famous ______________________________ in London – ____________

______________________ – a lot of people go to Knightsbridge.

There you can see ____________________ on a ___________________________, the

colours of __________________________________

Harrods is said to be the ____ in

Europe. There are around ______________________________ sales departments in

Harrods including the famous food halls.

Its motto is ______ ____

If there is something _________________, it will be _________________ and delivered

____.

Questions on the text:
1. What's the name of the famous shopping street in London?
2. Where is Harrods?
3. What are the colours of Harrods?
4. How many sales departments has Harrods got?
5. What is Harrods' motto?
6. Where do they deliver?

SHOPPING

LET'S GO SHOPPING

You want to buy something in a shop or a stall in a street market in London.

- Match the English sentences on this page with the German sentences on the worksheet and write them down in the correct place.
- Compare your solution with the answer key.
- Find a partner. Learn the sentences together and act out the scene.

  Tip: The scene will be better if you use real things, like books ...
- Change roles.

Material: rolecards, worksheet, answer key

That's ....

It's ....

What can I do for you?

Here you are.

Thank you. Have a nice day. Good-bye.

Here you are.

How much is it?

No, thank you.

I'd like to have some ....

Good afternoon.

Anything else?

LET'S GO SHOPPING

shop assistant	you
Guten Tag. Was kann ich für Sie tun?	
____________________ ____________________	Ich möchte ..., bitte. ____________________
Bitte schön, noch etwas? ____________________	Nein danke. Was kostet das? ____________________
Das macht ... ____________________	Bitte schön. ____________________
Danke. Einen schönen Tag wünsche ich noch. ____________________	

A SHOPPING GAME

Let's play a game like the German *"Stadt-Land-Fluss"*.

- Play the game with two or three classmates.
- Everyone needs a list like the following one:

Points	fruit	vegetables	clothes	furniture

- One person says loud "A" and continues with the alphabet silently.
- A second person says "Stop!".
- Now you have to write down the name of a fruit, a vegetable ... starting with the letter mentioned.
- The one who has finished first says "Stop!"
- You will get the following points:
  - 20 points if nobody has the same word in this column (= *Spalte*)
  - 10 points if no one has the same word in this column
  - 5 points if someone else has the same word as you

Material: paper, pencil

THE VEHICLE PUZZLE

London has got a very good public transport system. You can get around by several means of transport.

- Look at the word-cards and the texts on the board. Are there words you don't know? Look them up in the dictionary.
- Each word on the word-cards corresponds to a text on the board. Put the right word-card on the board.
- Turn them upside down after you put down all the word-cards.
- If you put the word-cards down correctly, you will see a complete picture.

Material: word-cards, board, dictionary

THE VEHICLE PUZZLE – WORD-CARDS

British Rail (BR)

taxi

double-decker

tube

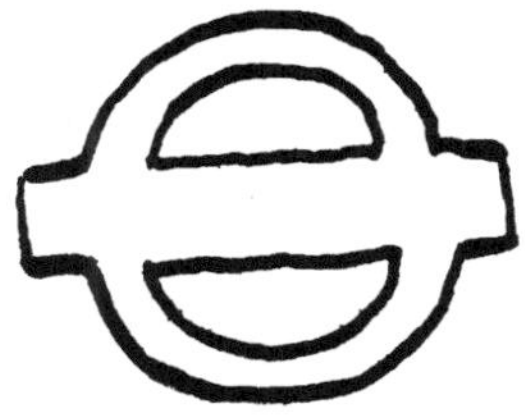

underground

plane

omnibus

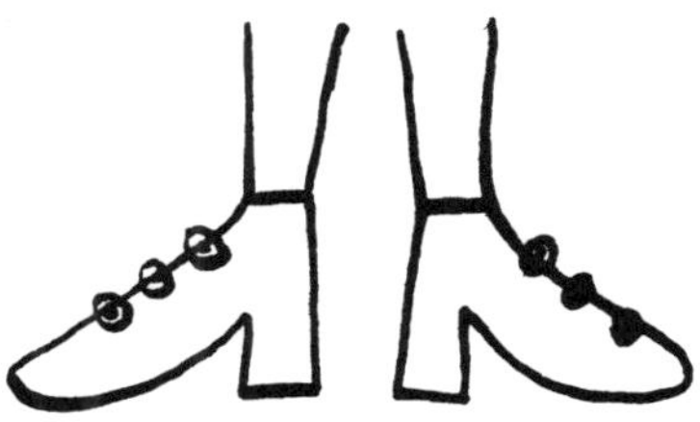

feet

boat

THE VEHICLE PUZZLE – BOARD

In this bus you can sit upstairs and downstairs.	In London most of them are black. They are called "cab" too.	What we call "Deutsche Bundesbahn" in Germany is called ______________ in Britain. It runs overground train services in all parts of Britain.
Near London there are five airports: Luton, Heathrow, City-Airport, Gatwick and Stansted. Heathrow and the City-Airport are close to the town-centre. If you come to London by __________ you will land on one of these airports.	You can travel through London under the streets by ______________.	Another word for "Underground" is ______________.
You can go on a sightseeing tour on the river Thames by ______________.	If you walk you don't use a vehicle but your ______________.	The first ______________ drove through London in 1829. Nowadays a lot of them are double-deckers.

TRANSPORT

STATION D2

GOING BY UNDERGROUND

The City of London built the world's first Underground in 1863.
The London Underground is very famous.

- Find the following Underground Lines on the map:
  a. The District Line
  b. The Jubilee Line
  c. The Bakerloo Line
  d. The Metropolitan Line

- Name at least one terminal station of these Underground lines.

- Imagine you are at Piccadilly Station and you want to go to
  – Tower Bridge
  – Westminster Abbey
  – Harrods

How do you get there? Name all the Underground stations on your way. Write them down. Do you have to change (= umsteigen)? Write down where you will change and what the terminal station of the new line is. Be careful or you might go in the wrong direction!

One example
From Piccadilly Circus to Notting Hill Gate:
"At Piccadilly Circus I take the Bakerloo Line in the direction of Queen's Park.
At Oxford Circus I change to the Central Line in the direction of Ealing Broadway.
Passing the stations Bond Street, Marble Arch, Lancaster Gate and Queensway I'll get to Notting Hill Gate."

- Show your teacher what you wrote down.

Material: map of the London Underground

GOING BY UNDERGROUND – MAP

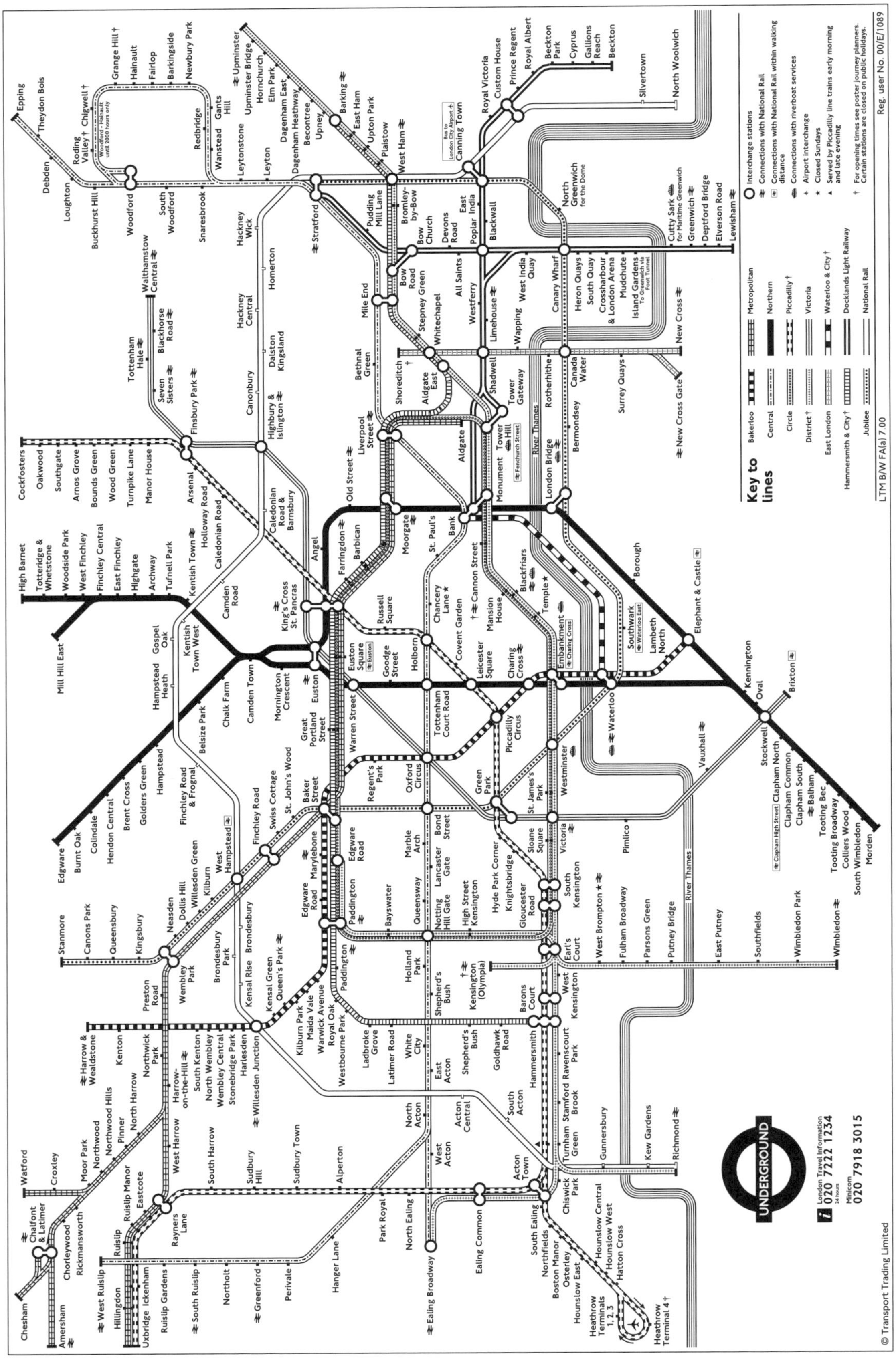

IN THE UNDERGROUND

- Read the text "In the Underground".
- Look up the unknown words and write them into your exercise book.
- Sort the sentence-cards according to the text.
- Read one sentence, keep it in mind and try to write it into your exercise book without looking at it again.

Material: text, cards

IN THE UNDERGROUND – TEXT

Martin and James were in the Underground. They were going to the London Transport Museum. At Green Park Station a young man got on the train and sat near the boys. He got off at the next station. But he left something on the seat. It was a green bag. James looked at the signs about bags. Perhaps there was a bomb in the bag?

The train started. Suddenly James jumped up and pulled the emergency brake. The train stopped quickly and everybody looked at the two boys. "Oh James, what have you done now?" Martin asked. When the guard arrived, he pointed to the green bag. "Somebody left his bag here."
"Don't touch it," the guard said. "Everybody get off the train and leave the platform. You two boys come with me. I'll phone the police."

The boys went to the station office in the street. After five minutes the police came. One policeman waited with the boys and asked questions. Some other policemen went to the train. Twenty minutes later a policeman came into the office. He was smiling. "Here's your bomb," he said. He put a box of cassettes on the table.

"I'm very sorry," said James. "Perhaps I've seen too many detective films."
"We saw the warning sign in the train," said Martin.
"It said 'pull the emergency brake' – and that's what we did."
"You did the right thing," said the policeman.

James and Martin left the station office.
Martin looked at his watch. "It's half past three," he said. "Come on, James.
We can still go to the Transport Museum."
"All right," said James, "– but let's go by bus."

TRANSPORT

STATION D3

IN THE UNDERGROUND – SENTENCE CARDS

Martin and James went to the London Transport Museum by Underground.
At Green Park Station a young man got on the train.
At Piccadilly Circus Station the young man got off.
He left a green bag in the Underground.
James thought there was a bomb in the bag.
He pulled the emergency brake.
Everybody looked at the two boys.
The guard told the people to get off the train and called the police.
The policemen looked for the bag.
Twenty minutes later they returned.
There were cassettes in the bag.
James was very sorry about pulling the brake.
But the policeman thought they had done the right thing.

TRANSPORT

STATION D4

ASKING FOR INFORMATION AND BUYING A TICKET

Travellers can get special travel information at the following stations: EUSTON, HEATHROW CENTRAL, KING'S CROSS, OXFORD CIRCUS, PICCADILLY CIRCUS, ST. JAMES'S PARK and VICTORIA.

You are in Piccadilly Circus Station and you need some information.

- Read the conversation.
- Change the marked words, so that you'll get a new dialogue. Use the expressions in the boxes
- Write down the dialogues in your exercise book.
- Learn the sentences.
- Act out the scene with a partner.

Material: worksheet, exercise-book

ASKING FOR INFORMATION AND BUYING A TICKET

"Excuse me, which **bus** do I take to Victoria Avenue?"	**train – Underground** Oxford Street, Buckingham Gate, Tower Hill
"Victoria Avenue? You have to take a **number 2 or 6 bus.**"	**the Underground to St. James's Park – the train to Fenchurch Street**
"And how much is it?"	
"Single or return?"	
"Single, please."	return
"It's **£ 1.10.**"	**£ 2.85**
"When does the next bus leave?"	train – Underground
"It leaves **at 11:20.**"	**at 2 o'clock** (train) – **in 10 minutes** (Underground)
"And where does it leave from?"	
"From the bus-stop round the corner."	platform 6 (Underground) – Euston Station platform 1 (train)
"Thank you very much, bye."	

A TOUR THROUGH LONDON

Let's go on a sightseeing tour through London!

- Play with your classmates.
- Throw the dice and move the correct number of spaces.
- Whenever you land on a question space someone takes a question card and asks you a question. If the answer is correct throw the dice again. If the answer is wrong you have to go back three spaces.

Material: game, dice, counter (= *Spielstein*), question cards

TRANSPORT

A TOUR THROUGH LONDON – QUESTION CARDS

What colour are London buses? Red	You can travel from place to place under the streets of London on the ... Underground
Most of the buses have got seats upstairs and downstairs. What's the word for a bus like this? Double-decker	Euston, Victoria, Paddington and Waterloo are all ... Underground stations.
Is it true that London taxis are brown? No, it isn't, the taxis are black.	Here are the first halves of the names – name the other halves. Piccadilly? Buckingham? Circus Palace
What word goes with these two names: Hyde? Regent's? Park	What is Madame Tussaud's? It's a museum of waxworks.
Where in London can you find the Beefeaters? At the Tower of London.	The London Underground is also called ...? Tube
Who are the Londoners? The people of London.	What's the capital of Great Britain? London
What river runs through London? The River Thames	Who lives in Buckingham Palace? The Queen.

TRANSPORT A TOUR THROUGH LONDON

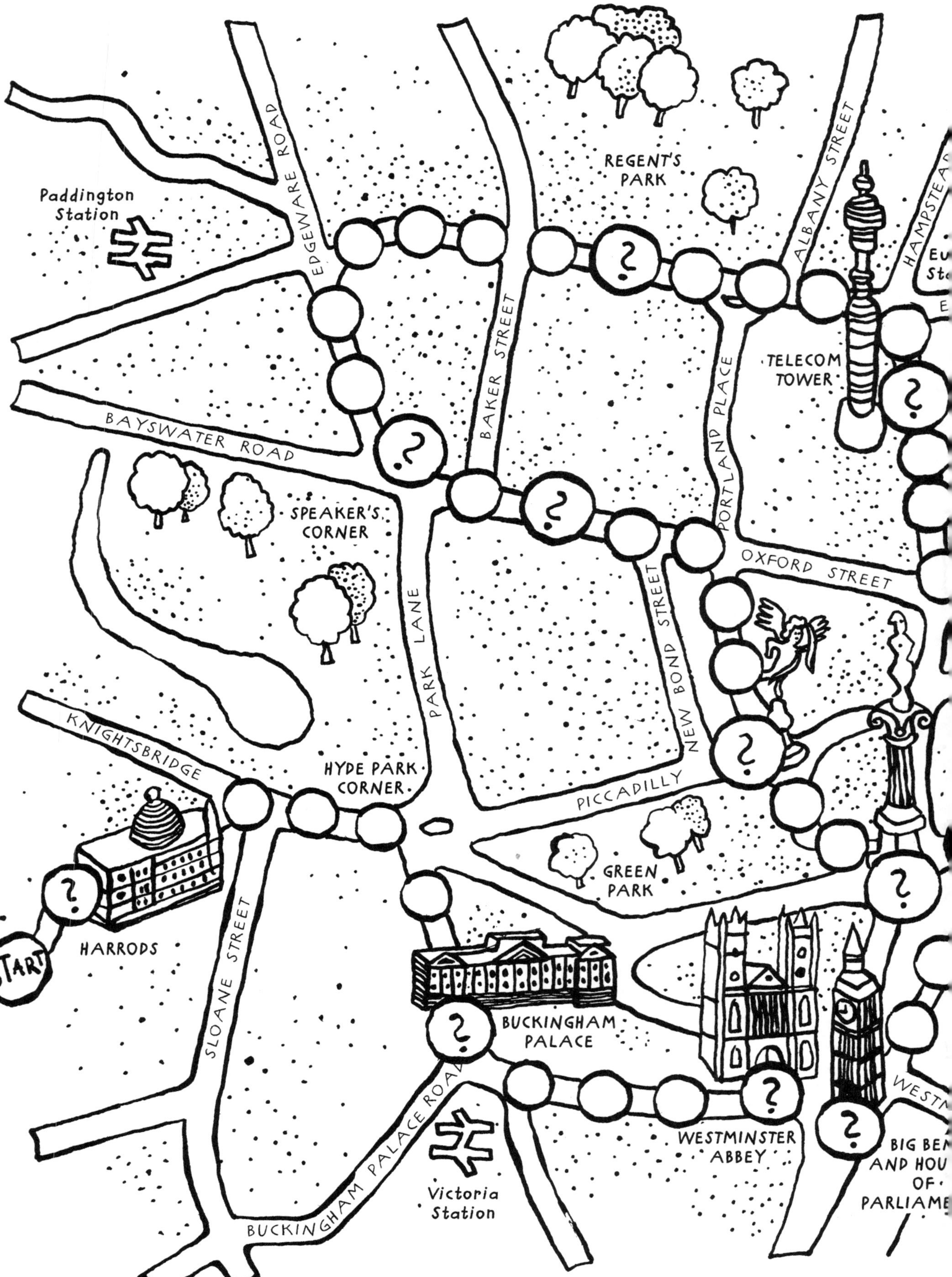

GAME BOARD

STATION D5

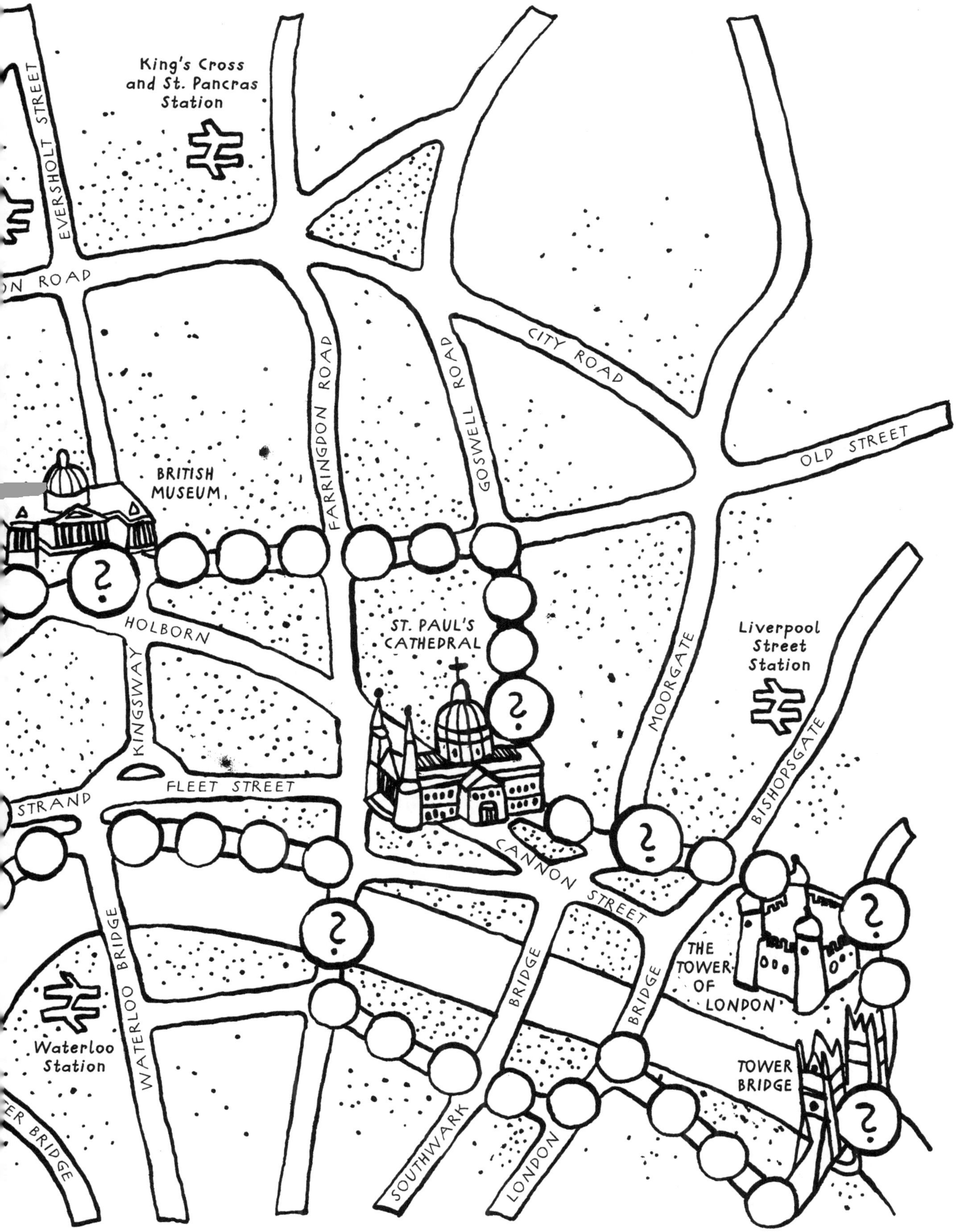

TRANSPORT

STATION D5

A TOUR THROUGH LONDON – QUESTION CARDS

What's the name of the world's second largest church? St. Paul's Cathedral	Famous Kings and Queens were crowned in this church. What's it called? Westminster Abbey
In Regent's Park you can visit another attraction! London Zoo	It has two sections which can be raised to let boats through. What is it? Tower Bridge
Once it was a prison, but now you can see the Crown Jewels there. The Tower of London	How do you know that The Queen is at home in Buckingham Palace? You can see the Royal Standard
It's called "the centre of London". Piccadilly Circus	Where do British politicians debate? In the Houses of Parliament
The famous bell inside the tower of the Houses of Parliament is called … Big Ben	Every evening people all over Britain can hear the sound of the bell "Big Ben". When? When the BBC news begins
Where do people meet on Sunday mornings to listen to speakers? At Speaker's Corner (Hyde Park)	What column can you see in Trafalgar Square? Nelson's Column
Is it true? London Bridge is now in America. It is true! An American bought it in the 1960s and took it to the USA	Do you know the name of a London street market? E.g. Portobello Road, Petticoat Lane …